The O

Classroom Questions

A SCENE BY SCENE TEACHING GUIDE

Amy Farrell

SCENE BY SCENE
ENNISKERRY, IRELAND

Scene by Scene
11 Millfield, Enniskerry
Wicklow, Ireland.
www.scenebysceneguides.com

Ordering Information:
info@scenebysceneguides.com

The Outsiders Classroom Questions/Amy Farrell. —1st ed.
ISBN 978-1-910949-15-3

Contents

Chapter One

1.   Why does the speaker like watching movies alone?

2.   Describe the speaker.

3.   What is a 'greaser'?

4.   Who, or what, are 'socs'?

5.   What is the speaker's family situation like?

6.   What happens when the five socs jump the speaker?

7.   Describe Darry, Ponyboy's brother.

8.   Describe Soda, Ponyboy's brother.

9.   How does Ponyboy react to being 'jumped'? How would you react in this situation, do you think?

10.   Describe the other members of the gang.

11.   What kind of girls do the gang go out with?

12.   Is life tough for Ponyboy and his brothers?

13.   What plans does Sodapop have for the future?

Chapter Two

1. What is The Dingo like? What do you learn about Ponyboy from his description of The Dingo?

2. What is your view of the way Dally tries to embarrass the two girls by talking "awful dirty"?

3. Describe Cherry.

4. Based on what you learn in this chapter, describe Dally Winston. Use examples to support the points you make.

5. "When you're a gang, you stick up for the members..." Is there sense in what Ponyboy is saying here?

6. Why is Two-Bit not concerned that Tim Shepard is looking to fight Dally?

7. Why does Ponyboy admire Two-Bit here? What does it tell you about Ponyboy?

8. Describe Johnny's injuries when the Socs beat him up.

9. What did the Socs do to him? What impact has this had on Johnny? Do you think his reaction is understandable, given his circumstances?

10. What point does Cherry make to Ponyboy about Socs and Greasers? Do you agree with her?

11. Do Ponyboy and Johnny have much experience with girls?

12. What aspects of the story interest you so far?

Chapter Three

1. According to Cherry, what makes greasers different to Socs?

2. Are you surprised the boys from the gang are getting on so well with Cherry and Marcia?

3. What makes Ponyboy make a mean comment about Johnny not being wanted at home?

4. How does Two-Bit respond to Ponyboy's comment? What is your view of this?

5. "We have all the rough breaks!" Do the greasers have a hard life, in your opinion?

6. Before she gets in the blue Mustang, Cherry tells Ponyboy she won't acknowledge him in school. What is your reaction to this?

7. Does Cherry's comment about falling in love with Dallas surprise you? What does it tell you about her personality?

8. Why does Two-Bit tear up Marcia's phone number? Is he right to do this, in your opinion?

9.   What makes Ponyboy resent the Socs so much?

10.   How does Ponyboy imagine life in the country?

11.   How do you feel when Johnny says he'll stay out all night?

12.   Does Darry over-react when Ponyboy comes home at two in the morning?
Do you understand why he behaves as he does?

13.   What makes Ponyboy run away?
What is your reaction to this?

14.   How does Johnny describe his life at home?
What is your reaction to this?

Chapter Four

1. What goes wrong for the boys when they get to the park?

2. What comment really gets to Ponyboy?
   Why does it get to him?

3. What does Johnny do while Ponyboy's being held underwater in the fountain?

4. Looking back on the story, were you expecting something like this to happen? Explain your view.

5. Did you think Johnny was capable of doing something like this?

6. Do you think the boys' plan to run away is a good one?

7. "I studied Dally." What is Ponyboy's assessment of his friend?

8. What do you think of the way Dally helps Johnny and Ponyboy? Is he looking out for them?

9. What, do you think, might happen next?

10. What does Ponyboy realise about their appearance, once they jump from the train?

11.   How do you imagine Darry and Sodapop will react when Dally tells them what happened?

12.   The speaker mentions a "creepy feeling" and a sense of "premonition" in the final paragraph of this chapter. What impact does this have on you, the reader?

Chapter Five

1.   Ponyboy describes a usual weekend morning as he
        wishes he were at home. Does it sound like a good start
        to the day, in your opinion?

2.   Ponyboy seems very stressed out as he waits for Johnny
        to return with supplies. Why is this? How would you
        feel in his position?

3.   How will the boys disguise themselves?

4.   According to Johnny, why do guys like them have to get
        their hair cut if they're in trouble with the law?
        Is there any truth in this, in your opinion?

5.   What does Ponyboy think of his new appearance?

6.   Are the boys coping well under the circumstances, in your
        opinion?

7.   Are Ponyboy and Johnny lucky to have each other here?
        How would it be different if another member of the gang
        was there?

8.   What is your reaction to Sodapop's letter to Ponyboy?

9.   Is Dally a good friend? Explain your viewpoint.

10.   What's happening between the Greasers and Socs as a result of Johnny killing that kid?

11.   Who is Dally's spy? What is your reaction to this?

Chapter Six

1. Why is Cherry helping them?
   Would you help them, in her position?

2. Are you surprised when Johnny says he wants to turn himself in?

3. Johnny asks Dally about his parents. Does this surprise you, given his bad relationship with them?

4. Why is Ponyboy glad to go back?

5. What new side does Ponyboy see to Dally as he drives them home?

6. What happened at the church while the boys were at the Dairy Queen?

7. Why does Ponyboy run into the church?

8. Describe the scene at the church.

9. How does Johnny deal with the fire?
   Does he surprise you here?

10. Why does Dally stop Ponyboy going back for Johnny?
    What is your reaction to this?

11.   What injuries do the boys sustain in the fire?

12.   The author makes us think that Dally was leaving Johnny inside and prevented Ponyboy from saving him. Then we learn he went back in to save him. Why does the author 'trick' us like this?

13.   What view does Jerry have of the boys?
        Do you think he cares that they are greasers?

14.   If you were Ponyboy, would you tell Jerry all this information about yourself and the gang?
        Why does he do this, do you think?

15.   "Suddenly I realized, horrified, that Darry was crying."
        Does Darry's reaction here surprise you?

16.   How do you feel as the chapter ends?

Chapter Seven

1. What got Ponyboy so confused as they waited to hear how Dally and Johnny were?

2. The reporters seem very interested in the boys. Is this good news material, in your opinion?

3. Describe the injuries Johnny and Dally sustained. What is your reaction to how they've been hurt?

4. Ponyboy imagines a bleak future for Johnny. How accurate is he here, in your opinion?

5. Why is it important to the greasers not to show their emotions? Is this still true for teenagers today?

6. What do you learn about Ponyboy and his brothers as he prepares breakfast?

7. What do you think of the headline in the newspaper?

8. Ponyboy learns from the newspaper that he will have to appear in juvenile court. What is your reaction to this?

9. Ponyboy is worried that he and Soda could be sent to a "boys home or something". If you worked for Social

Services, what would you recommend for the
Curtis family?

10.   Why has Soda's girlfriend gone to live with her grand-
mother in Florida? What is your reaction to this?

11.   Why does Ponyboy want to clean the house?
Does this tell you anything about his personality?

12.   According to Randy, what was wrong in Bob's life that
made him act as he did? Do you agree with Randy's view?
Explain your answer.

13.   Is Randy a coward to avoid the rumble? Explain.

14.   Ponyboy sees Randy as a guy, not just a Soc. What does
this tell you about Ponyboy?

Chapter Eight

1.   Describe Johnny's condition.

2.   Johnny refuses to see his mother. Does this surprise you?

3.   Describe Johnny's mother.

4.   What do you think Dally intends to do with Two-Bit's switchblade?

5.   Two-Bit says the only thing that keeps Darry from being a Soc is the gang. Does this make sense to you? Why is the author making this point now?

6.   "I had the same deathly fear that something was going to happen that none of us could stop."
What is the mood like in this chapter?

7.   Are you surprised that Cherry Valance won't visit Johnny?

8.   "You're a traitor to your own kind and not loyal to us."
Ponyboy seems to understand Cherry, yet speaks spitefully to her here. What makes him do this?

Chapter Nine

1. "The rumble was set for seven." Does it surprise you that this is a pre-planned, arranged event?

2. Ponyboy isn't feeling well before the rumble. Why do you think this is?

3. What reasons do the gang have for liking fights? What is your reaction to this?

4. The boys say a lot of negative things about Greasers as they get psyched up for the rumble. Why do they do this?

5. Describe Tim Shepard.

6. Imagine you are a movie director. Who would you like to cast as the main characters in this story? Explain your choices.

7. Why does Ponyboy think Darry is better than the rest of them? Do you agree with him?

8. Tim is proud of his brother in reformatory school and praises Ponyboy and Johnny for killing the Soc. What do you think of this?

9.   Ponyboy thinks the Brumly boys "have weird vocabularies". Does this strike you as funny at all?

10.   "We're greasers, but not hoods, and we don't belong with this bunch…" Explain what makes Ponyboy say this.

11.   Ponyboy feels that Greasers and Socs are judged by their looks. Is it true that we judge people by appearances? Why is this the case?

12.   What is significant about Paul, the Soc who takes Darry on to start the fight?

13.   Describe the rumble.

14.   Are the boys badly injured in the rumble?

15.   Why does Dally now think he was crazy for wanting to keep Johnny out of trouble? What does this tell you about life for the Greasers?

16.   What do Johnny's dying words mean, in your opinion?

17.   Describe Dally's reaction to Johnny's death. Why does he react like this?

18.   Does the outcome of the rumble matter?

Chapter Ten

1.   What state is Ponyboy in as he breaks the news of
     Johnny's death to the gang?

2.   Dally phones Darry, looking for help after robbing
     a store. How do you feel this will end for Dally?

3.   Why does Dally raise his gun towards the cops?
     How does this make you feel?

4.   Ponyboy doesn't want to think about Johnny or Dally. Do
     you think he is coping well with his grief?

5.   Does Ponyboy have a good relationship with his brothers?
     Explain.

Chapter Eleven

1. Why does Ponyboy hope Bob's parents hate them? Why does he feel this way?

2. What bothers Ponyboy about his school friends coming to visit him?

3. Are you surprised by Randy's visit? Would you have gone to see Ponyboy, if you were Randy?

4. Ponyboy says some untrue things to Randy. What do you think is going on here?

Chapter Twelve

1. What is the outcome of Ponyboy's court case?

2. How is school for Ponyboy, after the hearing?

3. Are you surprised when Ponyboy threatens the three Socs with a broken bottle?

4. Why does Two-Bit tell Ponyboy, "don't get tough"?

5. What's unusual about how Sodapop's behaving? What do you think is going on?

6. Darry speaks about Dallas and Johnny to Ponyboy. Is he right to bring them up like this, in your opinion?

7. Are you surprised to hear that Soda feels torn between his brothers?

8. Why does Soda want his brothers to "stick together against everything"?

9. What happened with Soda and Sandy? What is your reaction to this?

10. What is your reaction to Johnny's letter?

11. Are you satisfied with the story's ending?

12.   Did you anticipate any events in the novel?
    What made you expect them?

13.   Does this story have a lesson or moral to it?

14.   What statement, if any, is the author trying to make
    about people?

15.   Is Johnny's advice to, 'stay gold', good advice?

16.   What does this novel teach us about challenging
    stereotypes?

17.   Does this novel teach us anything about friendship or
    loyalty? Explain.

Scene by Scene Series

WWW.SCENEBYSCENEGUIDES.COM

Good Night, Mr. Tom Classroom Questions

Martyn Pig Classroom Questions

Of Mice and Men Classroom Questions

Pride and Prejudice Classroom Questions

Private Peaceful Classroom Questions

The Fault in Our Stars Classroom Questions

The Old Man and the Sea Classroom Questions

The Outsiders Classroom Questions

To Kill a Mockingbird Classroom Questions

The Spinning Heart Classroom Questions

Visit www.scenebysceneguides.com to find out more about Scene by Scene Classroom Questions teaching guides and workbooks.

Lightning Source UK Ltd.
Milton Keynes UK
UKHW050752270121
377685UK00008B/284

9 781910 949153